T0365377

This book belongs to:

_____

Chosen By Love
Adoption

Rebekah Stion

WestBow Press books may be ordered through booksellers or by contacting:

WestBow Press
A Division of Thomas Nelson & Zondervan
1663 Liberty Drive
Bloomington, IN 47403
www.westbowpress.com
844-714-3454

ISBN: 979-8-3850-0766-0 (sc)
ISBN: 979-8-3850-0767-7 (hc)

Library of Congress Control Number: 2023917592

Print information available on the last page.

WestBow Press rev. date: 10/04/2023

WESTBOW
PRESS®
A DIVISION OF THOMAS NELSON
& ZONDERVAN

For
Matthew and Melissa

"How thankful I'll always be
For the moments spent with children
Treasuring the love they share with me."

Rebekah Stion

CHOSEN BY LOVE

ADOPTION

It was the last day of Vacation Bible School and Donna Bradshaw was excited as she brushed her long black hair. "This week has passed too quickly," thought Donna, as she placed the big red bow on top of her head.

The words that Mr. DuBose, her teacher, had written on the chalkboard the day before kept popping into her mind.

Tomorrow's Bible Lesson: God's Adoption Plan

The word ADOPTION had caught her attention. Donna knew something about adoption. Six years ago, when she was just a baby, she had been adopted. Donna could hardly wait to hear Mr. DuBose tell about God's Adoption Plan. Donna loved God and she enjoyed learning about him.

As she looked into the mirror she thought about her own adoption. Her mother and dad had always been truthful about her adoption. They told her that she had been a very special baby.

"But, Mother," Donna had asked, "how did you find me?"

"Well, Donna," Mother had answered, "first, your Dad and I had been praying for God to send us a baby. We believed that one day God would send a special baby for us to love. We heard about a place called the ADOPTION AGENCY in a nearby town.

6

"The adoption agency is a place of business that cares about children and their needs. Sometimes when a baby is born its birthmother or birthparents cannot provide proper care. The adoption agency helps find a home for the baby.

"Your Dad and I visited the adoption agency and the lady there was very nice. We told her that we wanted to adopt a baby for our very own. We filled out papers and asked her to let us know as soon as the agency knew of a baby for adoption.

"Three months passed and then one day we received a letter from the adoption agency. The letter said...

Dear Mr. & Mrs. Bradshaw:

Please call our office for an appointment. We have a three-day-old baby girl that needs a home. You are being given first choice.

Baby Girl   7 lbs. 8 oz.
Race   Oriental/Caucasian

"Your Dad and I talked to God for a long time that night. We wanted to do the right thing for the baby, for us, and for God, too. Then, the next day we made an appointment to see the baby.

"We went to the nursery at the town hospital. A nurse brought the baby for us to see. She was a beautiful baby, with thick black hair.

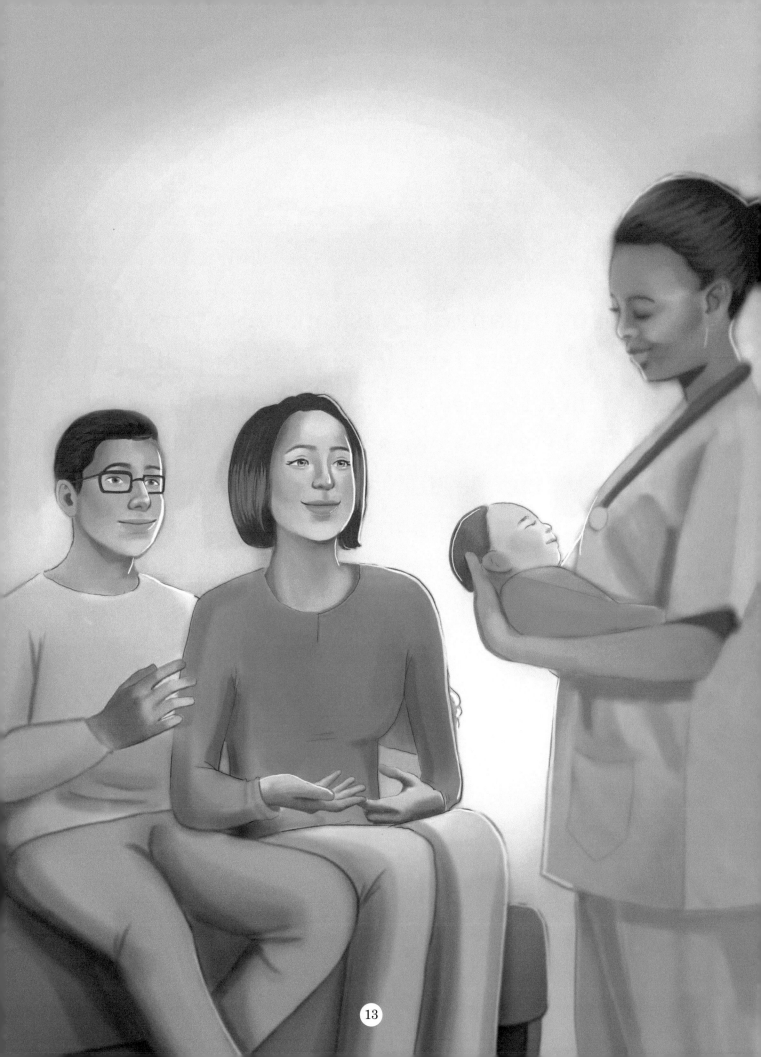

"The baby began to cry as the nurse handed her to me. I hugged her close, she stopped crying and opened her pretty brown eyes. I knew right away that she was our special baby. I whispered a thank you prayer to God. We had a home, food, clothing, and enough money to take care of her. But most of all, we loved her and wanted her to be our little girl. That little girl was you, Donna. We chose you because we loved you. You have our name and we are your mother and daddy for always."

Donna had liked it when her mother said always. That meant that no one could take her away. She took a final look into the mirror and then rushed from the bedroom. It was time to go to Bible School. Her mother and dad would be waiting for her.

Donna was glad that the church was only a five-minute drive from her house. From the back seat, she watched her mother and dad talking quietly to each other as the car rolled along toward the church. Donna had a happy heart as she thought about the last day of Vacation Bible School.

As soon as her dad parked the car Donna climbed out and ran toward her friends. Everyone had already formed a line in front of the church steps.

Mr. DuBose rang the hand bell as Donna reached the group. They marched eagerly to the classroom at the back of the church.

Everyone found their own special seat at the large table in the center of the room. They were excited about the day's activities!

"Boys and girls," spoke Mr. DuBose as he called the class to order. "The last day of Vacation Bible School has arrived. We'll begin with our Bible story, and then we'll go into the church dining hall for a delicious spaghetti dinner. The award certificates for attending Vacation Bible School will be given out after the meal."

Everyone cheered!

Mr. DuBose opened his Bible storybook and pointed to the words on the chalkboard. GOD'S ADOPTION PLAN

"Does anyone know what the word 'ADOPTION' means?" he asked.

No one spoke.

Donna sat very still. Her heart beat fast. She could feel everyone looking at her. They knew that she was adopted. It had never been a secret.

Donna hesitated for a moment, then raised her hand.

"Mr. DuBose," spoke Donna in a soft tone of voice. "I'm adopted. My mother and daddy said that adoption meant that I was special chosen because they wanted and loved me. Now we're a family and no one can take me away from them. I belong to them."

"Donna, you are right," exclaimed Mr. DuBose, with a happy smile. "Adoption is a special chosing. It is being wanted and loved by someone. Adoption is taking someone by choice to be your very own because you love them.

"In the Bible we are told that when God first made the world, love was with him. God was thinking about love when he made people like you and I. God not only loves everyone, he wants them to love him and become his children. That means that God wants to ADOPT himself a family."

Mr. DuBose held up a large poster board. On it was a picture of Jesus sitting in the middle of a group of children. Jesus had his arms around the children like a father hugs his children.

Donna smiled and joy filled her heart as Mr. DuBose talked about Jesus loving the children.

Donna thought about God's great love. She was glad that God had an adoption plan. She hoped that all the boys and girls in the world would accept his love in their heart.

As Donna bowed her head for the closing prayer, she had a new understanding of being CHOSEN BY LOVE. The last day of Vacation Bible School was the best day of all!

Printed in the United States
by Baker & Taylor Publisher Services